PREPARING
to PART
Love, Loss and Living

STEVEN SHEFTER

PREPARING
to PART
Love, Loss and Living

STEVEN SHEFTER

FIRST EDITION
Strong Life Publishing, LLC

In honor of Susan, the love of my life and my soulmate
And to our wonderful children and grandchildren

CONTENTS

Introduction xi

PART I: CARING FOR EACH OTHER 1

Sitting on Top 3

Order from Chaos 5

Managing Change 10

Living for Today 14

If Things Were Rough Before 17

Break from the Negative 20

Asking for Help 23

Remembrances 25

Without a Parachute 29

PART II: A NEW REALITY 33

Revised Order 35

Promises Made, Promises to Keep 38

Uncharted Road 41

No One Size Fits All 44

A Difficult Process 46

Not All at Once 48

A Broken Heart 50

365 Nights..52

Facing the Inevitable 56

Fingerprints..58

Where Did Everyone Go?..60

Dazed from Days..65

What's Next? (Re-Purposing Myself) 67

PART III: INEVITABLE CHANGE..73

Conquering Challenges...75

Problems and Pandemics 78

Reaction to a Pandemic..81

If You Know Someone Who Lost a Spouse or Other Loved One......86

Parting the Right Way 89

Endnote 90

INTRODUCTION

All my greatest accomplishments in life flowed from the love Susan and I had for each other. She was part of all my greatest joys; my happiness was better with her. If I was sad, that feeling was muted by her presence. If I was weak, I grew stronger being with her. Joys were doubled and sorrows cut in half knowing and loving her.

We did not have a perfect marriage—no one does. But it was a relationship our friends admire and our children wish to emulate.

Our marriage began August 8, 1982—the best day of my life. My other best days happened because of that one.

Then on January 29, 2019, I became a widower. Younger than I ever anticipated, more devastated than I could have imagined. It was the worst day of my life for it brought an end to our incredibly beautiful journey together.

It was 41 years since our first date, 36 years since we were married.

If I knew at the beginning how it would be at the end, I would do it all over. If this heavy grief is the price I have to pay for that life and love, I would say, "Sign me up!"

Shortly before my 50th birthday, we celebrated our 25th wedding anniversary. At that milestone, a young man at work asked me, "What's the bigger deal? Turning 50 or 25 years of marriage?"

Without hesitation, I answered, "Twenty-five years of marriage." To live to 50, you just have to live. But 25 years of marriage takes effort if you want to have a marriage worth celebrating. And that we did.

I am about to share with you the eight months of Susan's terminal illness. I am not going to talk with you about medical diagnoses or treatments.

Instead I will share how Susan and I took care of each other. She was not the patient with me as the caregiver. We were caregivers to each other. Though she was the person in the hospital bed, we were there for one another. My story is about how we made the best of a heartbreaking situation.

Why is this important?

As the surviving spouse, you have to carry the weight of everything that's happened—everything you did that was good and everything that went wrong. And you have to live with all this for the rest of your time on earth, facing it without your spouse.

Susan and I closed out our time together in a way that is allowing me to rebuild after the earthquake. We made this a meaningful ending so I am able to live without the guilt and regret that plague so many surviving spouses.

If reading this helps lighten your grief even slightly, I am happy I made this effort to capture what Susan taught me and what we learned together.

No one's path is perfect or straight, and no two people have the same journey. But we all have similar needs.

And so, this is how we were, *Preparing to Part.*

"We do not remember days;
we remember moments."

—Cesare Pavese

PART I:
CARING FOR EACH OTHER

SITTING ON TOP

"Happiness depends upon ourselves."—Aristotle

When our kids were little we would go to Cape May, New Jersey, for family vacations in the summer—ice cream, the beach, sand, rides and kite flying!

At the time, I said to Susan, "Wouldn't it be great if one day in the future we come here with our kids, their spouses and a bunch of grandchildren? What a dream that would be."

Now we were older and we had made it! The kids were married and we had a few grandkids.

We all celebrated my birthday with a family getaway in Cape May, 11 of us together, biking, flying kites, playing games, eating barbecue and ice cream. We were sitting on top of the world!

Then three weeks later news came crashing in, shattering our plans and destroying our future. Susan had a terminal illness. Not what I had in mind when envisioning the future.

Early in our relationship, Susan and I developed a personal communication style to handle challenges. When we couldn't agree on a solution to a problem, we would use the best out of five Rock Paper Scissors as a tie breaker.

For us, the game was not just a way to solve disagreements. It was a way to handle problems without making a big deal over something small or too big a deal over the big stuff. The key to our happiness was openness, honesty, and respect. Rock Paper Scissors just helped facilitate some of this. But with Susan's illness, life had become more complicated.

With the crisis we were now facing, we focused on trying to continue being the same couple we always were despite a challenge of this magnitude.

ORDER FROM CHAOS

"Just when I think I have learned the way to live, life changes."—Hugh Prather

What do you do when the love of your life is dying? Perhaps he or she was ill for a while so you saw it coming. Or maybe it came out of nowhere like it did in our case.

Either way, life has limitless possibilities one day; and on the next day, the end of all those possibilities is in sight.

So the question remains, what do you do? What do you say to each other and what do you do for one another? You're forced to face the unfathomable reality that your time as a couple is nearly over. And it's not impacting just the two of you. There may be children, parents, extended family and friends to consider, each with their own reactions to the situation.

Though the end is imminent, it's not here yet. Each day is a challenge and the idea of survival takes on new meaning. It's necessary for you to address the crisis as a couple, but you also have to address it alone, each in your own way. After all, one of you is dying but the other one is going to continue living. Your individual crises are vastly different.

When a plane is descending in crash mode, you are told to put an oxygen mask on yourself first, then to assist others who may need help. If you fail to survive, you're not in a position to help anyone else. With your spouse or partner dying, your plane is certainly crashing and you need to prepare yourself for impact. Of course, this is easier said than done.

I like to know where I'm going because I'm a meticulous planner. When I learned Susan had so little time left, it certainly threw me for a loop. I needed to talk with her, but this was an unexpected problem without a solution.

Susan and I were always good communicators, but that's not the case in all marriages, especially in times of crisis. Despite the devastating prognosis, we managed to tell each other we love and appreciated each other. I also assured her I would be there for her.

We talked and realized we were the same couple we were before her illness. But our circumstances had changed dramatically and we had to adapt to the new world order—a reality we didn't want and wished we could banish from our lives. But it was not going away.

Our 2,000 pound monster was Susan's terminal illness. For others it's a different monster, but in the end, all giant monsters bring the same result—death, destruction, or some other terrible fate.

Susan and I held hands, looked at each other, and committed to try and remain the same loving and dedicated couple we were to each other for 41 years. This was not a given, for serious illness distorts reality. As soon as you get used to the new normal, another new normal comes around that's usually worse.

I sought to assure Susan I would be there for her no matter what and she would not have to go through anything alone. This was especially important because she began having panic attacks during some of her treatments. I sought to reassure her. "Susan, my love," I'd say. "I will go through this with you for as long as we have together. And I will love you more at the end than I do right now."

She took comfort from my words and returned the favor in her last letter to me. She wrote: "For a couple like us, no amount of time together is enough." I will always treasure those words; they were her final gift to me.

Those of us who are survivors live with our actions, good and bad, forever. So it's important to do what you can to take care of your spouse or partner. By doing the right things, you ultimately take care of yourself. None of this is easy, in fact it's terribly hard, but along with being heartbroken, a small part of you will be proud of yourself. This is the price you have to pay for the love and joy you once had.

I'll give you some specifics, but remember that my actions were based on my marriage and my wife's needs. Yours will no doubt differ, but some details about what we did may help trigger your own ideas.

The guiding emotion at the beginning of any crisis is fear, in this case fear of losing your loved one. Fear can be so intense it turns into an obsession. Though the inevitable end is visibly down the road, you still have today. And it's important not to waste even one day living in debilitating fear.

The doctors may say your loved one has just three to six months to live. But they don't always get it right. What happens if your loved one beats the odds and lives for another decade? You want that life to be satisfying, so try to live in the present and not focus on fear of death and fear of parting.

Focus instead on love and holding hands, staying physically and emotionally connected for as long as you can. You'll have more than enough time to mourn your loss; so don't anticipate more than absolutely necessary ahead of time. Some early sadness is inevitable, but try to minimize it. And with medical science extending lives, and new treatments being developed all the time, you never know. Hold on to hope.

One way of accomplishing this is to do only the things you need to do, putting off spending precious time on anything that's unnecessary. Put things in a literal or figurative drawer if you can't do anything about them, or if they are simply unimportant.

Those unimportant things can wait. Of course, only you can decide what is or isn't important. Just try to avoid anything that distances you from your most important focus—the love the two of you share and your mutual concern for each other's well-being.

One man in my bereavement group, I'll call him Alex, is filled with remorse over his wife's car. Shortly after her dire diagnosis, he got it in his head he needed to get rid of her car. The vehicle was paid off and they were more than financially comfortable, but Alex decided the car had to go. This upset his wife but she didn't have the strength to argue with him about it.

Now that she has passed, he admits the act of selling her car when she took ill was ridiculous. It took time and energy that would have been better spent enjoying the few weeks she had left. It also sent a painful message to his spouse that her illness was truly hopeless. Though that turned out to be true, she didn't need to be reminded of the probability by losing her car.

No doubt her husband focused on the car because it was less painful than focusing on his wife's suffering. While that's understandable, he hurt both of them and he is living to regret it. I want you to avoid that kind of regret.

Alex also denied his wife of a measure of control. While she could no longer control her health despite her best efforts, something as simple as what to do with her vehicle should have been left to her.

Susan made a point to tell me she wanted to be in charge of all her medical decisions unless and until she was too ill to make them. She wanted to retain the power that comes with decision-making as long as possible. A terminal illness robs a patient of control. As the spouse of someone who is so ill, you want to treat your partner as a fully functioning adult with valid thoughts and opinions.

Discuss how to address day-to-day life issues. Will we go to the movies or stay home? Go out to eat by ourselves or with others? Can we still be intimate and how should we stay close?

Honor your spouse's needs and desires too. If he or she wants to be alone, is not in the mood to go out, or is not in the mood for intimacy, don't take it personally. You are both navigating uncharted waters and your spouse should be encouraged to be honest.

The goal is to make the best of the time you have left and to end that time together in love, not by arguing. Illness and stress often create distance. You want to do everything possible to span that distance and remain close, in whatever form that now takes.

MANAGING CHANGE

"I don't know that love changes. People change.
Circumstances change."—Nicholas Sparks

Susan and I loved going to the movies—romantic comedies, action movies, and thought provoking—it didn't matter. Three to four times a month, we would choose a movie to go see, share a container of popcorn, hold hands and enjoy the film. Then we would go out to dinner afterward. It was always a great date!

With her advancing illness, evenings out became increasingly difficult. So we changed up the entertainment. I would be at one end of the dining room table doing a 1,000 piece jigsaw puzzle. Susan was at the other end working on a complicated LEGO set.

I am an antsy person. If anyone ever said I would one day do huge puzzles, I would never have believed it. But all I wanted was for us to be together—and the puzzles afforded me that luxury.

Susan began losing strength in her hands. For her, putting LEGO pieces together was becoming nearly impossible. So I bought her a pair of small pliers and she was able to use those to apply pressure to the pieces. Those pliers let her continue the hobby and made her feel in control.

We sat for hours just being together. It was truly great and we both treasured the time as we made the best of what we could do. I ended up doing six 1,000 piece puzzles in eight months. Meanwhile Susan built a LEGO rocket. Her rocket is now prominently displayed in my living room—each piece a part of the time we spent together.

In the bereavement groups I've attended, almost everyone carries regrets about things not done and dreams not realized. These regrets are among the most painful aspects of losing a loved one. Keep that in mind, for this is not a time to wait for the good things you want to do. Whatever dreams your spouse may have, try to fulfill them. Maybe your spouse will live longer than expected, but you don't want to delay.

Susan always loved rockets, specifically Gemini rockets because her father worked on them at an aerospace company. She had fond memories as a child with her daddy learning about, and being amazed by, these rockets.

For several years, Susan looked for just the right Gemini model to build; but she never found the right one. I was always the hunter-gatherer when it came to buying things for our house, so one night after Susan became ill, I spent hours scouring the Internet for Gemini rocket models.

Thankfully, I finally found it—a LEGO rocket with 1,000 pieces, and that's what she ended up working on during our time together. Susan had never done a LEGO set before but she was excited about it. When it arrived, she painstakingly laid out all the pieces, and happily completed it with the help of the small pliers I bought for her.

While she worked on the rocket, she felt like a kid—creative and distracted from her illness. I was at the other end of the dining room table doing a puzzle. We had good quality time fitting into the limits of her illness.

I was able to help Susan realize her dream of building the rocket and displaying it in the house. Her excitement and appreciation are things I will always treasure. Whenever I look at the LEGO rocket in the living room, it is a forever memory of Susan. It brings me joy for having found the kit and reminds me of her joy in completing it.

This is a time of little things, little pieces of sand that fill up your time together and leave you with tender moments and wonderful memories.

Illness is harsh and takes away a patient's dignity at times. Tender moments are treasures to fill up whatever time is left and help you feel connected to one another. The closeness you gain may actually make parting harder in the short term, but it will make the long term easier. There is no downside for giving and receiving love.

Most serious illnesses reduce the capability to do day-to-day tasks, meaning increased work and added responsibilities for the healthier spouse. This is a given you have to accept. If you aren't flexible, you will break. Even if it wasn't your style before, try to roll with the punches, making the transitions easier.

While your spouse or partner is still alive, continue to live normally as much as possible. If you stop doing what you enjoy, it's like dying twice. So encourage each other. If you try and fail, at least you tried.

Susan and I planned a trip to New York a few months before she passed. If we gave into our initial feelings of despair, the trip would not have happened and we would have missed out.

While there we got to see one of our favorite entertainers, Elton John, at Madison Square Garden. I will forever cherish the memory of that trip. For more than two hours at the concert, we forgot about the illness and had a great time. We even bought silly LED Elton John eyeglasses and later gave them to our grandsons.

As much as we wanted to fly to Australia to see koalas and hike another national park, these activities were not feasible within the confines of her illness. But we did make it to New York. And truthfully, all we really wanted was to be us, to be together and see our children, grandchildren, friends and family.

We talked a lot during this time also. I asked her questions that bothered me and she asked me some too—little things for which I now have an answer, little things I could resolve for her as well.

In such a dire circumstance, I recommend you learn to adapt. If, as a couple, you love to walk, hike or bike and usually do five miles, be happy even if you can do just a few blocks. It's better than not doing it at all—again, you don't want to die twice.

Have great times within the limits of the illness. Hold on as long as you can, and maybe, just maybe, you'll have more time than the doctors expect.

LIVING FOR TODAY

"The past, present, and future mingle and pull us backward, forward, or fix us in the present."—Anaïs Nin

If you have a major doctor's appointment in two weeks, keep yourselves busy...and distracted. Worry is inevitable, but it's important to try to focus on the present.

Quite often reaction is a choice. A dear friend of mine is going through a similar situation. He tells me that he and his wife stay busy and distracted before BIG appointments. Their philosophy is, if the appointment goes well, then the dread leading up drained them of quality time. If results are bad, even horrific, they will process it after the meeting.

Not everyone can think this way, but it's worth trying.

It's also a good idea to avoid a "would a, should a, could a" mindset. It does nothing toward making the current situation palatable, and it robs you of time and energy. Whatever triggered this catastrophe, don't berate yourself for a lack of omniscience or omnipotence. Those qualities are reserved for the almighty or whatever higher power you may believe in.

Questions are good too—of doctors, lawyers, and clergy. Questions can help ensure your spouse or partner gets the best possible advice and care. But don't ask questions for which there are no answers—questions like "Why?" You'll just wear yourself out and drive yourself crazy.

Recognize that you're under tremendous stress and you may need to minimize triggers. I personally stopped watching the 11 o'clock news. I didn't want to end the day finding out how many people were shot, trapped in a fire, assaulted, or robbed.

I listened to soft music instead and stuck with light stuff—no more violent movies or television. The heaviness in my heart and the noise in my head calmed somewhat, allowing me to focus on my wife. This worked for me.

For others, watching the news or a thriller might be cathartic, providing an outlet for angst. It's important to know what works for you.

And yet, living for today doesn't mean ignoring what's ahead. It's unfair to your dying partner if you refuse to discuss practical matters. After all, he or she is still with you, wants to be heard, and needs to have a voice.

Susan and I took an hour one afternoon during one of her better days and went over banking stuff, as well as little things like club memberships and loyalty programs that were in her name. We even went through all her passwords and changed them to ones I would remember.

I was the one who lost it emotionally a few times, but we would hug and get past it. We moved on to going over her death benefits from work. She was proud her benefits would make my life a little easier. She had worked hard for many years and though she would not benefit herself, she was happy I would.

When I got emotional again, Susan said, "Steve, everything's going to work out. I have confidence in you." We had lived a beautiful life, but materialism was not one of our cornerstones. Her death benefits would certainly help, though I would have done anything to alter the course we were on.

There comes a point when you don't want to delay things you want to do. For example, calling a friend to tell them your spouse is not doing well and informing them a visit would be welcome. No matter how much someone cares, they want to be respectful and will take their cue from you. Often they don't know what to do and want guidance.

One of Susan's oldest and dearest friends came to see her after traveling a long distance to get here. Her visit produced some wonderful moments and brought the two long-time friends closure in a beautiful way. A call from me precipitated the visit but Susan's friend incurred the time and expense to make the trip, as well as the emotional expenditure it cost her. But her visit to Susan was a priceless gift and I will forever be grateful.

IF THINGS WERE ROUGH BEFORE

"The best way out is always through."—Robert Frost

I am frequently asked if what I'm advising applies to your situation if there are significant existing challenges in your marriage. How do you communicate during a crisis better than you did beforehand?

Perhaps one or both of you are poor listeners. Maybe your pattern has always been to yell and fight when confronted with problems and frustrations. Obviously, with your partner suffering from terminal illness, fighting is an impossible choice. Your strategy during this crisis must take into account that your partner will pass away. You, the surviving partner, will carry the weight of the imperfections from your relationship, including how you handle the time your spouse has left.

You're in a situation necessitating change from the past. Facing the new reality is a good first step to improving your relationship even under the most difficult stress.

Focus on what attracted you to your spouse both in the early part of your relationship and later on—the excitement and passion during your time together. Focus on positive aspects with the understanding that no relationship is perfect. The past isn't going to disappear, but that goes for the good as well as the bad.

With regard to trying times, you can't change what may have happened. But perhaps now is a good time to say, "I'm sorry" for a wrong or misunderstanding that went uncorrected. Focus on the love you have and on making the most of the time you have left.

If you're in the habit of saying, "I love you," make sure to continue the practice. Pulling away or distancing yourself at this time is something you'll regret later, so hang in there. The three words, "I love you" are among the most powerful ones we have. If you have not said them frequently enough before, saying the words now will mean more than you can imagine.

"Thank you for our life together," is another set of powerful words.

Remember that every relationship has ups and downs. You can't undo difficulties, but most of them likely don't matter at this point in time. If you can't fix something, push it to the side for both your benefits. You want your spouse to be at peace now that the end is close. Agitation doesn't help anyone. And as the surviving spouse, a calm and loving ending will play a significant role in how well you will be able to rebuild after your loss.

I knew a couple who had a 40-year marriage during which both spouses were known for yelling and screaming. When they fought, walls would rattle. But when you saw them walking down the street they were always holding hands. Then one day the two had a fight just before the husband went in for a minor surgical procedure. During surgery an aneurysm burst and the husband went into a coma for three weeks before passing.

The wife lived for ten years after that and felt guilty the entire time about the fight. Guilt is an insidious emotion that can destroy your happiness. As difficult as it is to keep composure during a crisis, it's important to rise to the occasion and be the best caring person you can be. Otherwise you may live to regret it and I don't want that for you.

Time is too short and precious to spend your time looking in the rear view mirror at past wrongs and hurt feelings. Focus on positive memories and loving feelings instead.

BREAK FROM
THE NEGATIVE

*"No act of kindness no matter how small
is ever wasted."*—Aesop

Sometimes the harder you try to avoid something, the more it seems to come after you, smacking you across the face. This is the case when you're dealing with delicate situations and feelings related to death and loss.

In trying to make the best of our situation, we made a huge effort to relax and enjoy ourselves. The times we went out to the movies, we tried to only see lighthearted films. When we watched television, we gravitated toward baking and cooking shows. After all, no one was going to choke to death on a croissant.

Even so, death became an unavoidable topic because of our situation. It was seemingly everywhere now that we were face to face with it.

One activity I did to keep myself distracted was to write. I was not in the mood for much in the way of comedy, but I liked writing poems and songs. I also liked coming up with alternative words for popular songs. This gave me a creative outlet as a break from the challenges surrounding me.

A few months into Susan's illness, I was sitting with her during one of her treatments. To distract myself, I wrote the lyrics for a song based on what we were going through, and I thought it was a great song. Titled "The Valley," my lyrics covered our life together dipping into a valley and hopefully coming out the other side.

I am a big James Taylor fan and I'm on one of his mailing lists. As I finished writing my song, an email showed up on my phone about an upcoming show James was producing along with a note that read: SEND JAMES AN EMAIL.

I took this as a sign from heaven so I wrote a message to James Taylor about Susan and me, and our story, offering to send him the words to my song. I figured, why not? So I wrote the email and promptly clicked, SEND.

To my amazement, two days later I received an email response from James Taylor! OMG, I couldn't believe it! I knew it wasn't really from James Taylor but from someone who responds to his emails, but still I could not believe it.

The response read as follows:

"We thank you for the beautiful story about you and your wife. It is touching. Regarding the offer of your song, unfortunately James does not accept music from others but we thank you. Perhaps we can send you something from James. We wish you well!

Wait, it gets better!

Two days later I received a UPS envelope sent from Massachusetts. I said, "Susan, I think I got a letter from James Taylor." I opened the letter and inside was a signed piece of sheet music, "Secret O' Life." It read: *To Susan,* and was signed *James Taylor.*

I couldn't believe it. He signed the sheet music and the song selection was uncanny. He didn't send "Fire and Rain." He sent a song I've sung 100 times and yet never before realized what it meant. The selection could not have been more perfect. Susan and I cried, but they were happy tears.

I have always been a James Taylor fan, but now I'm even more so. I still have the sheet music he sent; it's framed and resides in a prominent place in my living room.

ASKING FOR HELP

"You don't have to do it all by yourself."—Elizabeth Dehn

If you need help and you don't ask for it, you're isolating yourself.

If you were head coach of an NFL football team, you'd recruit players of different sizes, shapes and skills to fill out your team.

Well, within two weeks of Susan's diagnosis, I realized I couldn't manage this nightmare in a vacuum. I needed help. Susan needed help.

I decided to develop a team to help me help Susan, help my family and myself. I could not rely on Susan like I had in the past because she was so ill. And the truth of the matter was I needed a team because Susan wasn't going to be here in however many months.

I'm an independent person and asking for help doesn't come naturally to me. But this wasn't a natural situation.

I needed assistance with Susan's medical care. I needed to know there were people who could wisely guide me while Susan was ill and help me with the harrowing task of managing life when she was gone.

Early on, Susan told me she always hoped I would go first because she knew she would be better at managing the loneliness and difficulties of being the surviving spouse. No, she didn't want to bump me off, she was just realistic.

Because of what she said, I was especially motivated to prove to her I could handle this and I would be okay. Even though she was ill, she was looking out for me and I was determined to reassure her.

The team I put together was composed of friends and advisors whom I admire and respect. These were individuals who were good listeners, smart, wise, and accessible to me. They didn't always agree with me, but that was what I needed—people with perspective.

They complemented my strengths and weaknesses, almost always responding when I needed them. These were the people I went to first when things were good and when things went bad.

REMEMBRANCES

"The moments we share are the moments we keep forever."—unknown

As time was drawing to an end for Susan, she said to me, "Steve, I'm afraid I will be forgotten. I'm afraid the family won't remember me and there will be no way for our grandchildren now, and any future ones, to know about me."

I told her, "Susan my love, you will be remembered every day. You will be spoken of every day by me and our children. And your memory will be conveyed to our family. I promise you."

But I knew she was not satisfied with that answer. Neither was I.

I wanted Susan to know her life would be remembered for generations to come. She made a 75 minute video for our children, but that wasn't enough.

Around this time I read about the impending death of somebody well known who was afraid he would be forgotten. If a famous person was afraid no one would remember him, how could any of us not worry about the same thing? I wanted Susan to be at ease, to let her know she is and will always be appreciated and adored. So I came up with an idea.

Throughout her illness, Susan received many cards from friends, family, and coworkers expressing prayers, love, and appreciation. I compiled all the notes and letters, and asked her coworkers and others to request additional notes for Susan. In two weeks, we had more than 50 letters. A week later we had 85.

Susan's condition was deteriorating and I wanted her to know how she would be remembered. I did not ask my children to participate in this project. They would write letters to their mother separately—letters that would remain private.

On a cold winter evening, the house was quiet. Susan was tired and she was finding it harder to express emotion.

I said, "Susan, I want you to know about a project the children and I are working on. We have compiled 85 letters written to you from friends and family—letters of love, caring and devotion sharing what you mean to them, what you've done for them, and how your memory will carry on—that your soul will forever remain in their hearts. The book is called *What Susan Means to Me.*"

I gave her the first 35 letters and told her I wanted her to see for herself what our children, grandchildren and great-grandchildren will have in their homes. In a quiet voice, she said, "This is a dream come true." We hugged as if we never wanted to let go.

She went upstairs to rest. I went into the den and wept uncontrollably.

Later, when I was calm, I wrote the cover page to the book—a love note, my last to her.

Our oldest daughter jumped into frantic task mode; she got photographs, layout, and spiral binding for the book done in record time.

A few weeks later, my children and I presented Susan with the final book, *What Susan Means to Me.* We were in our bedroom. Susan had a beautiful pale but weary smile and a look of contentment. She got to see the book.

Five days later she passed.

Not everyone will want to compile letters and notes into a book. After all, other priorities may get in the way, or perhaps many of your friends and loved ones are already gone and thus unable to participate. Maybe health issues get in the way, taking priority. Perhaps it's just not your style.

There are other ways to memorialize a loved one. The person who is ill can videotape messages to kids and grandchildren like Susan did. She even sang, "Puff the Magic Dragon," for the amusement of our grandchildren.

Our son did a video interview of questions he wanted to ask his mom. The questions were about the family history and her personal history.

After Susan passed, my children and I each picked out a favorite piece of clothing and had a teddy bear made for each of us and each of the grandchildren.

We also did a clothing drive in Susan's memory, collecting dozens of bags of clothing for a homeless shelter.

Letters can be written by the person who is ill too—letters to be opened later, perhaps on a birthday, graduation, or wedding day.

If you want your ill spouse to feel good, or a surviving spouse to have something special, framing a special photo or memento like concert tickets or a menu from a favorite restaurant, can be done by anyone who wants to help.

If your loved one was active in a cause, donating money for a plaque somewhere important in that person's name is something that lasts a long time. And if your loved one collected things of interest to a museum, attaching their name to the collection and donating it is a way to keep their name and memory alive.

In retrospect, there are things I wish I had done, but I was too busy in the whirlwind. I wish we sat down with an iPad or iPhone and just recorded us talking to each other, for instance.

However, life gets in the way, especially when you're in crisis mode. And some may not want to admit their time with a loved one is coming to an end. But maybe you'll have more time than you think—doctors don't always get it right. And recording yourselves might prove to be fun.

Find a way of creating additional memories if you can. That is the greatest gift you can give one another.

Whatever you do, don't be hard on yourself if you don't get to do any of these things. That's not the point. The point is to make things easier now and going forward. These are merely suggestions.

Everyone lives their lives differently, and every relationship is different.

WITHOUT A PARACHUTE

"Every little thing counts in a crisis."—Jawaharlal Nehru

There's no blueprint for how to land on your feet in this crisis. One of the ways we coped was to talk about the happy memories we shared.

Susan would talk about her hesitation to date me because of the height issue—she was 1.5 inches taller than me. I bought taller shoes and she wore flats—our first problem solved.

We remembered the first time I told her, "I love you." It was on a bridge at Rutgers College where we were students. She was excited and shocked by my words. It took her three days to reciprocate—that was a long three days for me.

Everything we did back then was a cause for happy conversation now—the day we opened a joint savings account, when I met her parents and she met mine, our wedding, moving into our first apartment together after the wedding, and the births of our three children.

Susan was an amazing wife, mother, daughter, sister, and medical social worker who wore the letters LCSW for Licensed Clinical Social Worker as a badge of honor. She was the Mom social worker at the hospital where she worked, getting all the difficult cases no one else could solve.

After working late, she would always say, "I am helping someone who is having the worst day of their life." During my worst day after she was gone, I didn't have the social worker I had loved for more than four decades.

Susan was a gifted listener more than a talker. Upon walking into a situation, she had the ability to absorb feelings and make them her own. She knew what to say because she understood how others felt.

When the horrendous diagnosis came, Susan immediately called a family meeting, contacting siblings, children, and key friends. She knew the diagnosis was bad beyond measure, but kept her composure. Her immediate concern was not just about her own health but also the stress it would have on our family and others. She was always the social worker.

As time progressed, she shared that she was not mad at God. She'd had a wonderful life, terrific parents, siblings, a loving husband, children, and grandchildren. She didn't know why this happened to her but she did not react with anger.

Always open and honest about her feelings, she continued to be so throughout her illness. She never lashed out at me and was always appreciative of the care and attention I gave her. If I made a mistake, she did not jump all over me. She knew I have a gentle soul and never used that to push any buttons.

She continually praised me for the care I gave her, wondering where I got the strength to stay by her side, be patient, listen, and try to anticipate her needs. She knew and appreciated that I shielded her from lots of extraneous things going on.

For example, one night at the hospital they forgot to make her IV food. As a result, she would have to go for more than 30 hours without nutrition. She was asleep as hours passed and the hospital admitted they made a mistake.

I spent three hours running around advocating for her in order to get this fixed. She didn't know about it until after it was resolved.

At home Susan knew the devastating effect this would have on all of us and made sure everything we did was acknowledged with a warm hug and kiss, plus the words, "I love you and I'm grateful you are by my side." She strengthened everyone who helped her with kindness and gratitude. This increased our resolve to help and care for her. We'll carry her appreciation in our hearts forever.

Even toward the end when things got harder, she continued to say good-bye in beautiful ways. In the process, I found abilities I never thought I'd have—patience to sit still by her side for hours, and nursing skills like hooking up and emptying catheter bags and administering IV feedings.

These things scared the heck out of me, but she would say, "I don't know how you are doing what you're doing, but I am so appreciative you're taking care of me." Thankfully, our youngest daughter is a nurse, and her knowledge and skill were a major source of strength to all of us.

I was taking care of the love of my life as she was losing her life, yet she made me feel like I was her knight in shining armor. She knew that no matter what, holding my hand was the treatment for my anxiety. She knew when I needed a break, and she knew when I needed a hug or a smile.

These may seem like little things, but in the thick of this mess, she knew my heart was breaking and she wanted me to have the strength not to be totally devastated when she passed. She kept saying, "Steve, you will be all right." I can write what I am sharing now because I want to show how a social worker dies. Susan didn't want to take anyone down with her. Instead she did a lot to care for me even during her illness.

When a person is drowning and the lifeguard goes to the rescue, the first thing the drowning person does is lunge toward the lifeguard and almost takes their savior down with them. Not Susan. She built me and our children up so we'd be proud of the care we gave her and not have any guilt.

Susan knew how to die in a way that allows her family to live.

PART II:
A NEW REALITY

REVISED ORDER

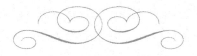

"If we don't change, we don't grow. If we don't grow, we aren't really living."—Gail Sheehy

If you've ever tried to fold an eight-foot tablecloth by yourself, it's not easy. That's 96 inches of cloth. No matter how hard you try to fold it in half then in half again, it just never folds right. That's because it's a two-person job.

Well, that's what life is like in many ways after the dust settles and you're back home by yourself—no longer part of a couple. Some difficult tasks are nearly impossible to do. Other things, simple ones, are hard because they are the tasks previously handled by your spouse. Those little things, like making the bed, cooking and food shopping, add up to a big heartache.

Life is filled with lots of little things. If you have two jars—one filled with rocks and the other with sand—the jar with sand weighs more than the one filled with rocks. That's because small grains of sand fill the entire space of the jar, leaving very little air.

It's definitely the small things that add up to a rich relationship—one that we cherish even long after our loved one is gone.

Terminal illness is frightening, but so is the thought your spouse or partner might die suddenly in the night or in a fatal car accident. There are no guarantees so it's vital you talk about the big and little things in advance, no matter how difficult the conversation. For if you've discussed what to do and how to do it in advance, decisions and actions are a little bit easier—you already know how to handle them.

A major shock to me was the first time I took care of two of my grandsons while my daughter and son-in-law went away for a few days. The boys were seven and four, certainly a handful but wonderful.

When Susan and I watched the boys, we had a division of labor. Susan did the bedtime routine—brushing teeth, reading, and singing songs. I took care of making letter-shaped pancakes with their initials, playing monster, and other goofy stuff.

The first night without Susan to help, I got panicky. Suddenly there was no division of labor and it was all on me—bathing the boys, bedtime tooth brushing, and less time for fun goofy stuff my grandsons and I enjoy. This caused a tremendous ache, but out of necessity, I quickly adjusted to the new world order. Suddenly doing a familiar task solo requires focus and rethinking.

It turned out I was capable of watching my grandsons. And though my own children are grown, I realize the loss of a parent is a hard reality no matter what their ages. As a result of their loss, I need to be the best dad I can be, even stepping up my game to a new, higher level. I cannot replace their mother but I can compensate by loving everyone a little more, listening longer to what they have to say, and hugging a few seconds longer.

My son suggested we look at all the roles Susan played in our lives to see if some of the special things she did might be filled in by others—perhaps another member of the family or a close family friend. This is not intended to replace his mother, but merely to solicit support.

The love Susan and I shared is the root of our family tree. Even with her passing, the tree continues to grow with new branches and leaves through my son and daughters, and through their children.

Just as Susan and I always hoped.

PROMISES MADE, PROMISES TO KEEP

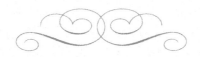

"My most brilliant achievement was my ability to be able to persuade my wife to marry me."—Winston Churchill

A constant theme of our conversations during Susan's illness was what she wanted for my future—that I have a happy, meaningful life. I reassured her I would do just that, but it's a tall order now that she's gone. She was the center of my world.

I'm going through the biggest crisis of my life and I need a hand to hold. But the hand I want is Susan's and it's gone.

For me, one of the beauties of being married was always having something to do. Being with Susan was something, even if we did nothing.

On a Saturday night, watching TV and sharing a pizza was something special when I shared it with someone I loved. Now Saturday nights are more of a challenge, but I work to plan my weekends far in advance to make sure I have something to do. I promised Susan I would be happy and I'm not about to break my promise to her.

Cooking is another challenge. I know how to shop and cook, in fact I'm good at it. Often I did the cooking instead of Susan. But cooking for one is not the same as cooking for others. Widows and widowers often fail to eat properly after their loss.

Eating with someone is social, so I'm inviting people over for a meal twice a month. And I'm making an effort to get out of the house other times and arrange to meet someone for lunch or dinner. Eating right is important for my health, and eating with others is important for my mental and emotional well-being.

I had lunch one afternoon with ten people, only two of whom I knew well. The two I knew came up to me after the meal and said, "You shared things about yourself we never knew." I realize that being alone so much gives me the impetus to talk more in social situations.

As a result, some friends have started reaching out to me more frequently. I guess I'm becoming a more interesting companion. Making the best of my situation is akin to making lemonade out of lemons.

Often I'm tempted to stay home by myself. I'm constantly trying to fight this inclination. While being a recluse would give me time alone to process my grief, there's such a thing as over-processing.

I've learned that managing grief is not like running a race in which the faster you grieve the sooner it will be over. Grief is a marathon with no exact beginning and no true endpoint. Perhaps it will never be over but it does become more manageable. At least that's what others tell me who have been dealing with this longer than I have. In the time since Susan's death, some aspects of my life have improved. So I am hopeful.

Then there are many people out there who are clueless. I went to dinner with friends recently and one person said to me, "Where's your wife?"

I said, "Excuse me?"

"Where's your wife?"

I said, "She passed away last year."

There was a pause and, "Oh, sorry. I forgot."

I try not to hang onto anger. I laugh inside and think to myself, this person obviously didn't get the memo. Thoughtless though this kind of remark might be, I don't believe the person behind the words meant any harm. I am certain I must have unintentionally done something similar at one time.

People don't remember all the details in everyone's life. Those who are married, for example, often think everyone is part of a couple, until they are not.

When confronted with the unimaginable pain of others, I plan to do better in paying attention.

UNCHARTED ROAD

"If I could plant a flower for every time I miss you, I could walk through my garden forever."—unknown

It's 1 a.m. and I can't sleep.

Sleeping is a challenge since Susan passed.

Having someone with whom you share your house, your space, and your time is something I love and truly miss.

When you share your room with someone, your sleep has a pattern, a rhythm. You may go to sleep at the same time or you may go earlier and your spouse joins you later, but it's a given...until it's not.

When your spouse is no longer physically there, you're faced with empty space.

Sound, which travels and reverberates around the room, is a part of it. Your spouse is someone providing a surface upon which you bounce the sounds of your life. He or she absorbs your words and their responses come back to you.

With your spouse gone, it's like a tent with no walls. The sound travels away from you but it doesn't return. That's what makes it so hard to sleep, among other things—like a lack of touch. The quiet can be deafening.

I know Susan had trouble sleeping when I travelled for work. I rarely had that problem because Susan's job didn't require her to travel. Now I'm living as if Susan is on a permanent trip and she isn't coming back.

At times it's impossibly hard for me to get through a night. Other times it's less tough.

In talking to other widowers, I learned that some stayed away from their spouses during their final illnesses. Sometimes touching was painful, other times it was a pulling away for emotional reasons.

I held on to Susan during the most difficult of times. The memory gives me sadness but it also gives me warmth and a strong sense of comfort that we stayed close and didn't drift apart. A certain distancing might be a survival mechanism, but it's important to fight that overwhelming feeling and hold on.

Otherwise you'll live to regret it, and regrets are to be avoided at all costs. They last forever, after all, and there are no do-overs.

Late at night during those last days, Susan and I reminisced about when we met, challenges with the kids throughout the years, and shared personal moments. In a sense we were verbally reliving our lives like playing a tape over and over again or looking through a photo album.

Toward the end, I made a playlist of our favorite songs. We would listen to the music and verbally go through an inventory of our life together. Often Susan would nod off, but the music and conversation kept her calm and me too. I was in survival mode for Susan. I wanted to be what she needed. She deserved that.

I sleep easier now, when I *can* sleep, knowing we comforted each other. She took care of me and I took care of her.

I occasionally listen to the playlist when I need a good cry. There's nothing wrong with crying, whether you're a man or woman. Crying is important to get emotions out and it's not a sign of weakness; it's a sign of strength when you can express yourself and then put yourself back together.

If you're not the crying kind, that's okay too. There's no one way to grieve. Go with what feels right for you.

NO ONE SIZE FITS ALL

"True happiness consists not in the multitude of friends, but in their worth and choice."—Samuel Johnson

After a major loss, a feeling of being disoriented and without an anchor, floating aimlessly, is prevalent. It's especially difficult dealing with friends and their spouses. Getting together when you used to be four but are now down to three isn't easy.

Seven months after Susan passed I went hiking in the Rocky Mountains with wonderfully supportive college friends who knew us. Days were lovely, but going back to the hotel with a couple when I was alone proved tough. After decades with a partner, being solo was foreign to me.

You may not want to be a social butterfly, or even have it in you, but it's essential for you to stay close with your friends if you're going to recover. And many of these friends will be married.

When you go from being part of a couple to being a single, dynamics change and friendships are pushed off-balance. It's like a mobile above a baby's crib—all the characters are carefully balanced. With the loss of one, the mobile is out of whack and doesn't move properly.

Just don't take it personally if your friends are uncomfortable. It's human nature to avoid awkwardness.

One of my children thoughtfully arranged for a few friends to come to my house for a guys' dinner on my first birthday without Susan. That was one of the first times I felt hopeful, believing my life could get some balance.

New patterns with old friends…like reshuffling the deck. Baby steps… and every little bit helps.

A DIFFICULT PROCESS

"No one ever told me that grief felt so like fear."—C. S. Lewis

Bereavement is a long, difficult process. Obviously, the loss of a great love is something you'll carry with you always, but thankfully its level of intensity changes over time.

However, if you don't deal with grief, it will drag you down and keep you down for a long time. Of course, it's not easy. Your friends and family might love you, but the truth is they don't want to continuously hear your problems. Everyone has their own issues.

I've watched people try to avoid grief by throwing themselves into work at a crazy pace, eating like crazy or going on an austerity binge, excessively drinking or gambling, and everything else you can imagine. This never works. Eventually grief catches up with them—it can run faster and longer than its victims.

In a marathon, grief wins the gold medal.

A few weeks after Susan passed I was depressed, angry and lost. My doctor advised me to go for bereavement counseling. About a month after the funeral, I began individual therapy.

Many people, especially men, avoid counseling because it seems like an admission of weakness. They want to think they are strong and don't need help. Likely they've never used counseling before and believe that in a few weeks or months, their bad time will resolve itself.

Unlike many others, I went for counseling as soon as I could. Nothing in my life had ever come close to losing Susan, not even a close second. And despite her death, I had responsibilities to my family, work, and to myself. I needed to get myself steady and functioning as soon as possible. And I was nowhere near where I needed to be.

Instead I was frightened, lonely, an emotional wreck and a functioning mess. If there was someone trained to help me navigate this sea of turbulence and change, I was ready to sign up.

And that's what I did.

I was fortunate to hit it off with the first counselor I tried. Not everyone is so lucky. Sometimes you have to switch counselors a few times to find one who relates in a way that works for you. In any case, the importance of having a trained therapist on your side cannot be overstated.

It definitely helps to acknowledge you're in emotional trouble and need help. For me, it was well worth the time and effort. No one size fits all, but I strongly recommend you make the effort yourself. Counseling is not the solution to everything, but it can help enough to make life manageable sooner rather than later.

Grief is a lonely road. The counselor helped me manage my loneliness and despair. No family member or friend could have done that.

I'm a spiritual person so I also sought counseling with a spiritual perspective, which provided additional insights and complemented my main therapy.

NOT ALL AT ONCE

"Sometimes, only one person is missing, and the whole world seems depopulated."—Alphonse de Lamartine

Support groups aren't recommended for at least three or four months. You're already overwhelmed and you're not ready to listen to anyone else's problems. So waiting awhile until the dust settles is a good idea.

When I finally did attend a support group, my interest started slowly. But after a few sessions, I started to appreciate them for providing a sense of belonging to a community of people going through what I was going through. It made me feel normal and gave me a social outlet for talking about my feelings with people who understood.

I also learned about other cultures' approaches to death and closure. Some were helpful, some were not to my liking, but to each his or her own.

I heard lots of stories. Some widows and widowers empty closets immediately; others turn their homes into a museum to their loved one.

Some start dating after just a few months, some wait several years, and some never date at all. One man started dating three months after losing his wife of 20 years. The woman he was dating said, "Let's get married" and suddenly the guy lost it.

"I'm not ready for this!" he shouted, and he ratcheted back to not dating at all.

Listening to survivors talking about selling houses, selling cars, fights with children, and other things, gives you ideas what to do and what not to do. Support groups definitely have their place, for you need a community— one that provides a safe, understanding environment.

I've been told I've made great progress and Susan would be proud. Starting at about six months after her death, I gradually started feeling better. It took time as well as effort and a willingness to accept that I was hurting. You can't cheat the process but you can make it more manageable.

I know Susan would not want me in pain a second longer than I need to be.

A BROKEN HEART

"Grief is like the ocean, it comes in waves ebbing and flowing. Sometimes the water is calm, and sometimes it is overwhelming. All we can do is learn to swim."—
Vicki Harrison

Today is a challenging day for many reasons. Lack of sleep and the anticipation of my first anniversary without Susan weigh heavily on me.

Tomorrow marks what would have been 37 years since we were married. I am blessed we had many wonderful years together. The price I have to pay for the fond memories and previous joy is much sadness. So be it.

I spoke with a friend this evening. He said my marriage is like a fine crystal goblet from which I enjoyed drinking, but it is now broken. I cannot use it anymore but I still remember enjoying the glass when it was whole.

I'm trying not to think too much about the anniversary as I plan a hike and dinner with a friend to celebrate the day, not to dread it. It turns out to be a good day and Susan would be happy for me

Life is not always fair but it is what we have and we must make the best of what we've been given. Sometimes good things can evolve from loss.

A woman I know lost her husband after a prolonged illness. She was worn out and emotionally drained from the ordeal. She had a cousin with whom she was once close, but their spouses didn't get along so the cousins' relationship ended.

Luckily the cousin reached out to the woman after the husband's death. That one phone call was the spark that rekindled their closeness. This doesn't always work, but it's worth a try. And don't worry about apologies for not calling. Just call. Old friends are like old trees, the roots are deep; but life gets busy, with the days turning into years so quickly.

A friend, a cousin, or a neighbor won't replace a spouse or partner of course, but the social interaction, the caring from another individual, certainly helps in the healing process.

One day at a time.

365 NIGHTS

"Courage is the power to let go of the familiar."
—Raymond Lindquist

Marking the end of the first year without a loved one is supposed to represent an end of the toughest time. After all, you've now gone through one complete cycle of birthdays, holidays, and anniversaries. Obviously it's been tough.

But does it actually get easier after that? That depends on your personality, on how you process grief, the other people in your life and so much more.

Your reality does change as you become adjusted to what—or rather whom—you thought you could not live without. You've survived 365 nights without a hug and kiss, without the words, "I love you and sleep well."

You've also survived 365 mornings without those same hugs and kisses.

I am a forward-looking person, but always with an eye on the past. I keep a paper appointment book with me at all times, in part because I am a paper person, in part because I like to look back and compare where I am to where I was previously. I've done this for years, long before Susan's illness, long before her death.

When I look back a year from today, I'm looking to see if life is better than it was right after the funeral, right at the start of the mourning process.

Well, life is different. In certain respects it's worse, in others about the same. And I am different. I miss Susan terribly but I've had to learn to accept the hand I was dealt. After one year, I recognize the differences in me through my re-purposing.

Before Susan, I was Steve 1.0. With Susan, I was Steve 2.0. And now I'm a new third version of myself—3.0.

So what's different about me?

I learned to become stronger in order to survive. And to once again find some measure of happiness, I had to open up and be vulnerable by allowing others to help me. I realized the necessity for sharing my feelings and asking for help when my friends and family didn't know I needed it.

As a married person, much of my world was a bubble with my wife. When that bubble burst, I had to figure out how to do things on my own, or find someone else to help. I could not afford to pity myself or accept pity from others. Only when I started to emerge from my shell did people start wanting to spend time with me. If I stayed home watching TV while eating ice cream and pizza, I would end up depressed, fat and falling apart.

In truth, people can only stand your grief for so long. They quickly grow tired and impatient, and they move on. As horrible as your loss is to you, to almost everyone else, it is yesterday's news. So you have to live for the future in front of you, not in the rear-view mirror.

I found the more I came out of my emotional pain and preoccupation, the more people were cheering me on to succeed. People love cheering for the underdog and people love when an underdog wins. Every day I go out, tell a little joke, go to a movie or out with a friend, is like one point in the win column. And this is what Susan wanted for me.

I am an obedient husband, even now. I've been thrown off the stage of my life; and instead of jumping back onstage, I first have to rewrite the script.

I went back to school and met many new people. It reminds me of when I was a freshman at Rutgers College many years ago. I had never seen the campus before I arrived for classes. So when I arrived, I put my things in my dorm but I didn't unpack. I just got out, started looking around and meeting people.

That is kind of where I am again, a lost freshman on an unfamiliar campus. I survived that scenario once; I can do it again.

I asked around to identify people who have gone through what I am experiencing. I met men and women with whom I share the link of loss. And I decided to go in a different direction in my career. Of course, this is easier to do, to take chances, when your kids are grown and independent. I'm in that situation and I need to do something different.

For others, the familiarity of a job and a career might be comforting. For me, I need to create a new purpose. The newness of change is helping me move forward.

I started writing, doing puppet shows for preschool children, and volunteer work for the hospice that was so helpful to me. I also started sharing my experience caring for Susan with others going through similar situations, in an effort to help them.

What I am writing today, I wish I had known when Susan took ill. It would have made my life easier. I've also become more aware of other people's crises and I'm trying to be a better person and friend.

The type of crisis I went through, and am still experiencing, can make you bitter or lead you in new directions. Faced with a harsh new reality that I can't do anything about, I'm learning to accept it and trying to maneuver to avoid the bumps along the way.

Thankfully I couldn't have done any more for Susan than I did. So guilt, other than survivor's guilt, is not an issue. Yet I could turn into a mean old angry man who was cheated out of his happiness. Or I can do what Susan asked me to do and have a happy, meaningful life, enjoying our children and grandchildren, and rebuilding my life. I can't do that if I am angry at the world.

As you prepare to part and the parting happens, know that you put a lot of time and effort into each other. No matter how many years I am blessed to be on this earth, the greatest tribute to the life Susan and I had together, and the love we shared, is for me to live a productive life.

It would be such a waste not to make the most out of the rest of my life, however long that is. It would be like building a house and not living in it.

Whatever your beliefs, mine let me hope to be reunited with Susan somehow. If that should happen, I would love to give her a big hug and kiss, and have her say, "Steve, I'm so proud of you! You took care of our children and grandchildren. You also took care of yourself and made the world a better place." I hope that will happen, but if it doesn't, I'll be gone and not know it.

Meanwhile, I'm looking forward.

FACING THE INEVITABLE

"Demons are like obedient dogs; they come when they are called."—Remy de Gourmont

Delaying painful triggers makes the demons bother you much longer. Realizing this, I determined not to delay my discomfort any longer for I know negative anticipation is often worse than an actual situation.

Susan worked at a local hospital for the past decade. Whenever I drove by the hospital complex after her death, the memories it triggered were hard to tackle. Yet this hospital was also the site of the birth of my three children and two of my grandchildren.

Since the hospital is in my neighborhood and it isn't going to disappear, I knew one day I would have to go there. So one day I did.

I went to the hospital and headed for its gift shop—a non-threatening place in the building. I bought a package of lemon shortbread cookies and an iced tea. Then I walked around the lobby for a few minutes, reliving good and bad times, grateful I didn't run into anyone I knew. I needed to absorb this visit on my own. And I left in less than 30 minutes.

Less than 30 minutes meant the parking was free. As I drove away, I felt tremendous relief. After dreading this visit for months, I finally got the nerve to go do it. I was relieved and I cried.

As a small reward for completing my mission, I ate the package of cookies and drank the iced tea.

Since then, it's been easier to pass by the hospital.

FINGERPRINTS

"Anything is possible when you have the right people there to support you."—Misty Copeland

There are billions of people on earth and no two have the same fingerprints. Susan left hers on my heart. What a gift!

At some point I realized no one would ever fully understand what I was feeling and going through. But I desperately wanted someone who could understand my pain. Besides the professional counselors I was using, I was looking for what I call, "a grieving buddy."

I found such a friend in a support group I attended. She comes as close as anyone to understanding my journey. This friend lost her husband and found coming to terms with that loss quite difficult. We alternated between which one of us was having the tougher day, but we understood one another. She has become a dear friend.

I also became friends with a fellow widower who is smart, kind, and sensitive. He is a great man and his participation in my life is a blessing.

In truth, there is no easy way to manage the challenges and transitions you're going to face. If you're so inclined, I'd recommend searching for a grieving buddy. I was fortunate to find two—one of each gender. They make a huge difference in my life and the friendships are continuing.

Be patient when attending a support group. At first most of you will probably say, "This isn't for me." But keep going if you feel ready for it. My support group allowed me to find a grieving buddy and it gave me a window into other perspectives and ideas on how to rebalance my world.

You'll no doubt hear a lot about attendees' views of religion and politics. You'll see anger and you'll hear about situations worse than your own.

Some people take years before they join a support group, others a few months, and some never do. The time it will take you to heal or even to begin the process of healing is individual to you. Don't let anyone tell you when you "should be ready" or even how you should do it. I'm only making suggestions; you'll know what's right for you.

The truth is you'll never completely get over your loss, but you will come to terms with it so the loss becomes manageable.

WHERE DID EVERYONE GO?

"Things change. And friends leave. Life doesn't stop for anybody."—Stephen Chbosky

When your spouse is terminally ill, you're dealing with many issues and various personalities on both sides of your family and in your social circle. Each person is reacting and grieving in his or her own way. Some family members and friends will be a fantastic source of help and comfort. Then there are those who will let you down in a big way. This is perplexing and infuriating, and you may become angry.

There are two stages to the support you will receive: (1) help and support when you are together as a couple, (2) and then once your spouse passes. In the second stage, it all changes.

After your spouse is gone, much will depend on relationships with both sides of the family. If children are involved, support will hopefully increase. This is important because the children have lost a parent; but to lose an entire side of the family can be particularly devastating.

If you are empty nesters, loss of your spouse's family will make things harder, so you should reach out to those individuals. Hopefully they will be there for you. After all, your spouse's relatives are grieving too.

The same applies to friends. Some are yours, some are your spouse's, and some belong to both.

Managing your support base is one of the most important aspects of getting through your life now and in the future.

Unfortunately, there are people you have known for decades who are going to let you down. This applies to both family and friends. Whether or not you were there for them during their problems and trials, many will *not* be there for you. You were there during their worst times so where are they now?

I've learned most people have no idea what you're going through. They just don't.

And then you have to battle the unintentionally insensitive things people say. "Don't think about what you lost, think about what you had," is one such remark. If I hear that one more time I will lose my mind!

My response to some is, "You can only live on yesterday so long."

In truth, you will carry the love of your spouse with you the rest of your life. If you're lucky, you may find love once more, but it will not be the same. So despite that saying, the past may be comforting but it doesn't help get you through your current crisis.

If you're trying to comfort someone who just lost a spouse or other loved one, listening is usually a better tactic than repeating a well-worn and virtually useless adage. Additionally, avoid comparing a loss you may have gone through with that of a spouse (or any other loss for that matter).

It's important to understand something about human nature—people avoid uncomfortable situations. They don't know what to say so they may avoid you as if losing a spouse is contagious!

I was in my local supermarket shortly after Susan passed. People I knew actually turned their carts around to avoid my aisle. Apparently I made them uncomfortable, so they visibly avoided me. Perhaps this is understandable from not-so-close friends, but with regard to close friends, it's hard to fathom or accept. Though it's wrong, I've learned it's not malicious.

Often you'll have a friend who is perfect for fun times, or perhaps he or she is great for a conversation about sports or finance. But can this person handle a crisis? Do they know how to listen? And do they know you well enough to help you through the maze of difficulties you're caught in?

Though it's a cliché, it's apt: *We are given two ears and one mouth for a reason.* We are supposed to listen more than talk. Most people think the answer to support is talking but it's really active listening that's important. Susan was gifted in doing this for others. She was a good, empathetic listener. This was an asset in her work as a hospital social worker and it certainly helped pave the way in our relationship.

But many people can't do that.

Compare your life to a car accident on the highway. Imagine you just had a horrible crash and traffic is backed up for miles. Police and fire trucks with EMTs have arrived on scene and everyone driving by slows down to stare. They are attracted by the flashing lights and ambulance so they drive slowly in order to look at the wreck. Then they accelerate off to wherever they are headed.

But this is *your* life. Thankfully, you are standing next to your wrecked car, unhurt physically but devastated emotionally. Friends and family who disappear after the illness and death of your loved one are accelerating away. Their cars are undamaged and they fail to look in the rear-view mirror because there's plenty going on ahead.

Also, they are scared of you and your situation. They recognize what you and your spouse experienced is incredibly frightening. If they think about it too long, they're irrationally but humanly afraid it will become contagious.

Perhaps it could happen to them! They don't help you because doing so will make them feel vulnerable—something worth avoiding at all costs.

My friends keep asking, "Steve, how do you live alone?" And they ask, "How do you get through the day?" It's almost as if I'm the ghost of their future.

So what can you do? You have a few options.

If there's a friend or relative you really want and need, approach them. Acknowledge you're going through a terrible situation, that you're kind of drowning and need their help.

You can say something like, "I need your ear and wisdom. Can we meet for coffee?"

Or you can tell a friend, "Please send me a text once in a while. It would mean a lot right now." Or suggest, "I could use a dinner out. Would you join me? And please forgive me in advance if I'm too much to handle."

These remarks empower the other person by letting them know their assignment. And it's not asking too much. You're in effect making them feel part of your team rather than an outsider. You may even end up closer than before, which you will need as you start to rebuild. By providing your friend with reasonable and realistic expectations, the friend feels needed and important. That's good for both of you.

If this person can't handle such a minimal commitment of friendship, you'll know to seek support elsewhere. Just because they've been there for 20 years doesn't mean they're who you need now. When things return to whatever is your new normal, perhaps they'll be there then. Or maybe you won't want them anymore.

A simple analogy is if you have a toothache. Do you go to a psychiatrist or a dentist? Not every person with whom you partied when younger is the right friend for conversation after your spouse endures a painful medical procedure. You need emotionally strong, sensitive friends. No offense to those others, but this is when your heroes are front and center.

Remember there are those who run away as fast as they can when they see a fire.

Then there are those who run toward the fire. These are the first responders of your life—your best friends. They understand what to do, or at least they're willing to try, and they care enough to do what is needed.

Maybe they've been through it themselves. Or maybe it's just chemistry. Whatever it is, thank heaven for them. You need them and for some reason they want to be there for you.

Before your current crisis, you may have been terribly off in how you treated friends in their times of crisis. Maybe you previously lived a sheltered life or you were just lucky. Now you are no longer sheltered or lucky.

Perhaps you were insensitive to the heartache of those around you. Maybe you were not the friend or relation others needed you to be.

But you didn't know or understand. Now, when you come through your own trauma, you'll likely become a more caring, sensitive person. Take this away as a positive and be forgiving of others. Likely they are trying, while combating their own insecurities and fears.

DAZED FROM DAYS

"Everybody needs his memories. They keep the wolf of insignificance from the door."—Saul Bellow

What do you do on Mother's Day when that was your wife's favorite day? Or Father's Day or her birthday...maybe your anniversary?

As I write this in May, it's the day when I asked the most important question of my life about 40 years ago, "Susan, will you marry me?"

I'm sitting here thinking about Mother's Day two years ago. As usual we had flowers, balloons, extra pampering, favorite foods, and a present. We also did a family brunch for 15 to 20 people. I truly miss that. But the most important thing was THE CARD.

We are an expressive family. We could never work for Hallmark writing cards because we'd write a book on each card. My children and I would write words of love and appreciation to Susan.

Susan and I saved the cards from all the occasions; we had two big fancy boxes found at craft stores filled with every card we ever received. We could see the evolution of our family—children's handwriting as it evolved, and the words and emotions as they grew. Our love of their accomplishments and appreciation expanded as we grew our family and ourselves.

Since losing Susan, I have occasionally looked in the boxes. I wish we thought of doing this together before things got too difficult. If you save cards and letters and have the time, do yourself a favor and go down memory lane together. You'll laugh and cry and have a special bonding moment. If you haven't saved every card, read whatever you do have.

The special days certainly feel different now than before. But if I turned every one of these special days into days of remorse, it would transform beauty into sadness. And what a waste that would be!

When I have the chance, I share the boxes of memories with my children. Celebration of Susan's life and memory is challenging. But as time moves on, joy will come easier. Not easy but easier.

And I hope to experience new special days going forward.

WHAT'S NEXT?
(RE-PURPOSING MYSELF)

"The pessimist complains about the wind; the optimist expects it to change; the realist adjusts the sails."
—William Arthur Ward

The funeral is over; the turmoil is settling down.

My children are back in their homes. The friends and relatives who took a few days off left to return to their lives.

I am in my home of 34 years, without Susan. I look at the walls and they are flat and lifeless. All the beautiful sounds of our life together are gone.

What remains are remnants of Susan's illness—the medicine bottles, a last load of folded laundry, unused containers of Ensure in the refrigerator, feeding tubes. Also left are the books and magazines she never finished reading.

I could go on like this forever. What the heck am I supposed to do?

Others in my situation go back to work immediately. Some take time off. I had the luxury of having someone cover my job for an extended period so I could take care of Susan.

As a widower, I now have the empty space of time that is no longer filled by taking care of her. Our couple time is vacant too. Is my identity gone as well?

I loved being not just a husband but Susan's husband. I always felt I married up and she was the best thing that ever happened to me. I will always feel married to her spiritually.

With her absence, my roles have changed too. During her illness, I missed a lot of time with my children and grandchildren. Now I need to be more involved with them. My children lost one parent and I need to help them through their loss even while I suffer through mine.

During the first few weeks, I set up bereavement counseling. I also made doctors' appointments to get myself checked out. And I tried to get out of the house as much as possible.

The house was kind of a mess, so my children arranged for a cleaning service to erase the medical smells.

The house needed more than a good cleaning, but that was a start. In my bereavement reading, I learned it would be wise to make the house my own, to personalize it rather than turn it into a museum to my deceased wife. Experts also advise surviving spouses not to make major decisions like selling a house and moving during the first year. But I could certainly freshen up the house.

I didn't want to spend a lot of money, but painting is a reasonable way of remaking space. I had my bedroom walls painted a light pistachio. In the living and dining rooms, I had the painter use a favorite color of mine—adobe like the color prevalent in national parks. Finally, I got lighter window treatments from a home improvement store. These let morning light into the house, making it easier for me to get up in the morning.

None of this was expensive, but it made the house look cheerful, different, and uniquely mine. I made these changes with the intent of elevating my mood and it worked. When people come over, they comment how great the house looks and how proud Susan would be of me.

I also started doing some things I always wanted to do, but could not with Susan. She had asthma and couldn't tolerate scented candles. Now I went out and bought a few. I rearranged the photographs on the wall and added some new favorite pictures. By making the house look and smell different, I felt my mood improving.

While Susan was ill and I was busy with her care, we had a housekeeper come to the house. Now I have plenty of time and I like working with my hands, so I established a cleaning routine and I've pretty much kept up with it.

When spring came, I bought an ornamental bridge for the front lawn and painted it Susan's favorite colors—purple and pink. It is not intended as a memorial, just a way to feel her presence and beautify my home.

At first I was going to skip planting flowers this first year because of my mourning. But I pushed myself because Susan loved flowers and would not want me to overly mourn. And I love gardening so the physical activity and enjoyment helps me take care of myself.

It keeps the house from looking bleak and sad too. Even though I feel sad, I am determined to appear cheerful. I want to send the message to my children that we all need to go on living.

After all, I am a role model for my children and grandchildren. Grieving and living can and should coexist. They see me cry but they also see me laugh. In addition to being there for them, I need to let them know only I am responsible to pull myself out of my doldrums. While they can spend time with me, I want to remain in the parental role—to advise and comfort them, not the other way around.

I took a pottery class with my oldest daughter. It was relaxing, therapeutic, and a great bonding experience for my daughter and me.

I got rid of Susan's car. Even though my own car was relatively new, I got rid of it as well because it was the car in which Susan got sick, and that memory was painful. So I traded both of them in for another car that doesn't have difficult memories attached to it.

While taking my grandson to his preschool, his teacher told me I was welcome to come by anytime. I told her I could do a puppet show and when I did the first one the kids loved it. So I started doing children's puppet shows with the 15 hand puppets I have. It makes me feel alive when I get to see the faces of three year olds laughing. It's great medicine.

Part of my bereavement work entails journaling and sharing my feelings with my bereavement counselors. From my journal, the counselors learned my whole story. They said, "Steve, you need to share your story as a way to help others." That's in part how this book came about. I signed up for a writing course at the community college. I met some great people and I found that almost everyone wants to write a book but most don't have the knowledge or stamina.

The students in the writing class were mostly middle-aged or older, and many wanted to write about a loss in their lives. I came to the conclusion that if you reach middle age or beyond and are not grieving for something, you are extremely fortunate.

I've lost my parents, my in-laws who were an amazing second set of parents, a brother, and now my wife. I know about grief.

In class I made new friends and the instructor said, "Just write and get your ideas on paper." She is the editor of this book and without her it probably wouldn't exist. I also took an inventory of personality traits, including what I like and don't like to do. The test revealed I should be a writer—further validation for expressing myself in this way.

My world was upside down so I started rewriting the script. I go for bereavement counseling, go to school, and do puppet shows. I garden, write, exercise and volunteer too. I also started going to the movies again. And I spend more time with my children and grandchildren.

I started biking again as well. I stopped biking because Susan was having panic attacks. She was terrified of my getting hit by a car, for that happened to several people in our circle. Now I can bike again. I would rather Susan be here and I not ride, but that reality doesn't exist anymore.

I've learned to be gentle with myself. Grief has a beginning but the end is forever; you just learn to manage it.

Friends can help, but you must let them in. You have to want to heal, to stop looking back. Otherwise you risk missing what lies ahead. I'm still alive and I need to ensure my own happiness. I'm the only one who can; I'm the only one who will.

PART III:
INEVITABLE CHANGE

CONQUERING CHALLENGES

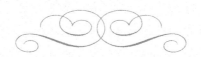

"Being challenged in life is inevitable, being defeated is optional."—Roger Crawford

Have you ever gone hiking with a heavy backpack on? Or have you watched a war movie in which soldiers are in a hot jungle, there's a torrential downpour, and they are each carrying a backpack weighing 75 pounds?

Going through life after loss is a lot like carrying a heavy backpack while hiking. And if you're able to find good counseling, it's akin to reaching a rest stop and dropping the weight of your pack onto the ground.

Most of us don't have the know-how to navigate the loss of a spouse or partner. After all, it's often a once-in-a-lifetime trauma. How can you possibly know how to cope with it if you've never experienced it before? It's much like taking a hike in which the weight gets heavier and heavier, and the path gets more jungle-like.

I went for counseling over the period of a year, starting with weekly sessions and tapering off as time went on. I did this because I was on a trail I'd never been on before and I needed a guide.

Susan and I loved hiking in national parks, so this analogy is particularly apt for me. We went to 17 parks and hoped to get to 50, but that just didn't work out for us.

Hiking is a perfect analogy, for it has so many ups and downs. The price you pay for the easy times going downhill is paid for by having to climb uphill on the other side. Sometimes you stumble and you're okay; at other times you take a nasty fall.

There's nothing like coming to the top of a climb and seeing a panoramic view. The funny thing about that view is once you get there, you spend a few minutes and then you start back. Isn't that crazy? You spend 7 hours climbing to the end of a trail and only 25 minutes enjoying the view before you start back. But it makes sense because you need plenty of energy to get back to the start.

Susan and I climbed to the top of a glacier in Alaska and it took 11 hours round trip. I was so sore afterward I could barely walk for a week, but the view was worth it—just like our life together was worth it.

When you look at marriage and other relationships in your life, they are all like a hike. I experienced losses before, but the loss of Susan was by far the hardest climb, one in which I fell and rolled down a steep incline.

As it turned out, my bereavement counselors were my guides, they were my Sherpas. They helped me manage the path, supplying oxygen as the heights got higher and the air got thinner. I cannot say they made the journey faster because this wasn't a speed race to the end. But they did help flatten the road.

The most important thing counseling did was to educate me that what I am experiencing is normal. The counselors gave me direction, encouraging me to be open, to share feelings, and be vulnerable so I could properly address my grief in an effective manner.

By addressing grief properly, I could be there for myself and for my children. I lost the love of my life, but I didn't want to lose my heart and soul to grief.

When issues arise, I occasionally go back for some additional counseling. Life can get complicated and if we fail to address things, we shove them into the attic of our minds. So every now and then I need to do what I call a little attic cleaning.

If you've never before gone for any kind of counseling, you might feel counseling is for the weak. I am not weak—I recognize my willingness to get the help I need is a sign of strength. Addressing issues early helps keep you strong and believe me, you are going to need all the strength you can get.

That's my thought.

PROBLEMS AND PANDEMICS

"Everyone thinks of changing the world, but no one thinks of changing himself."— Leo Tolstoy

I began work on this book informally about two years ago. As I have shared, there are always ups and downs on the road to forming a new world order. I cannot go back to the world I knew with Susan; although she is permanently part of my heart and soul, she is not physically with our family or me.

Every book has to have a last chapter and if anyone told me how I would conclude this one, and what I am about to share, I would have said, "On what planet are you talking about?"

Life is truly like writing a book. Neither is a linear process. You don't start like a children's dot-to-dot drawing, methodically going from point to point, and when done you have a picture to color of a dancing bear wearing a hat.

The saying, "Things can't get worse," is one I never use. For things can always get worse no matter how bad they are already. I'm not a pessimist; I'm a realist. Anyone who goes through a series of traumas and heartbreaks like me knows things can get worse before getting better.

Things eventually do get better through perseverance, determination, conviction, and often a little luck.

_____

In March 2020, the coronavirus pandemic spread from China to cover the world. The globe was filled with hundreds of thousands dead, millions sick, economic destruction, and the highest unemployment rate since the Great Depression. Everyone was forced to social distance by law. The consequences of violating the dictate were not mere fines or incarceration; illness and death were part of the equation too.

Emotional turmoil to some was catastrophic. Families locked together were fighting over what to watch on Netflix, where to get carryout, how to get groceries and basic necessities, how to keep children educated and out of trouble, and how to work at home along with their spouse—all to avoid illness or death.

For people like me, it wasn't the emotional turmoil of a house filled with people; it was the emotional turmoil of being alone. All the support systems I worked so hard to put in place as part of my rebuilding came to a crashing halt. It was as though I built a sandcastle on the beach and the coronavirus wave came and washed it all out to sea.

The support system of work, counseling, volunteering, and meetings with friends melted away, leaving me home alone and quarantined. I was part of a group at high risk for a bad outcome if I contracted the illness. And thus I was trapped.

Some people did Zoom meetings all day. That's fine for some, but for me it is much less satisfying than a face-to-face talk or a simple hug.

This may be a new normal, but it's anything but normal. No one knew how long things would continue like this, so I had to prepare a new plan for survival.

A few months earlier, I was fighting my way out of a grief pit, trying to rebalance my world. I worked hard to reach a new level of happiness and it was a tough challenge. But I would take the old new normal any day over what I was now experiencing.

Now I had to look at the last two years and use what I learned to start charting a new course once again. All the coping methods, bereavement counseling, and reorganization skills I learned needed to be reapplied to this new situation.

I experienced many difficulties since losing Susan. And the more time passed, the more I adjusted to facing difficulties and the unknown alone. I had started focusing on my ability to maneuver trials and tribulations since Susan passed. While not perfect, my confidence and competence had grown.

However, the world was becoming more and more distracted with the crisis at hand, and so was I. Problems that existed two months earlier became irrelevant for many, including me.

When you see millions of people lose their jobs, many thousands dead from the virus, families that can't make payments on cars, mortgages, rent, medical bills, and utilities, it makes you assess your situation in a different light.

I went through hell and back the last two years and felt this wasn't fair. How many setbacks could I handle? Heaven give me a break!

I did not take it personally that the pandemic was put on earth just to make my life worse. I didn't really think heaven would make the world of eight billion people miserable just to get at me. I may not be perfect, but I'm not *that* bad.

REACTION TO A PANDEMIC

"They always say time changes things, but you actually have to change them yourself."—Andy Warhol

As I did when Susan became ill, I set up a revised assessment of my world and a modified support system.

I live in a single family house where I can go outside and walk around without bumping into anyone infected. It's not as if I live in a city in Italy with the possibility of getting arrested for stepping outside. I have people to help me shop. There is a 24-hour donut shop drive-in if I need coffee or just to get out.

In summary, I'm a widower quarantined in my house. I miss my wife, my children, my work, and my friends.

But…I have a roof over my head, a smartphone, TV, 66 playlists on my Amazon Music, a computer, food in the fridge, and comfortable sweats.

In the scheme of things, my world was far from perfect but I could do a lot worse. A benefit of the recent traumas I survived is my training on how to handle challenging situations.

There's an old adage that if a group of people put all their problems, sorrows, and aggravations on a table, they would want to take their own problems back. There are always people whose shoes you'd rather be in and others you wouldn't want to get near.

Now that I recognized the problem, I needed a new plan.

I've always had trouble sitting still and when under stress, I like to organize and fix things. I'm not particularly organized, but with life out of order, all I wanted to do was deal with things I could get in order.

With the wave of the pandemic on its way, I got in preparatory shopping mode, buying things to keep me busy.

I planned to clean out the house I lived in with Susan for 35 years. Some say for every year in a house, you gain 1,000 pounds. Therefore, my house gained 35,000 pounds and I was putting it on a diet. I cleaned as if I was moving from a four bedroom house to a shack. And I used the rule of five—if you haven't used it in five years, get rid of it.

Then I decided to go with the rule of three years, then two, and then one year. In a few cases, I even used one month as a guideline. I bought six, 32-gallon garbage cans and 75 large trash bags.

There were numerous sentimental and emotional items I offered to my kids. If they didn't want something then off it went to Goodwill. Sometime in the future, my kids will appreciate what I've done because they won't have to do it themselves when I'm gone.

Next I bought paint for two rooms. I was quarantined so I bought the colors I wanted. Since I wasn't letting anyone into the house during a pandemic, decorator Steve got to make the color decisions. Months later a friend saw the colors and said, "How interesting!" In other words, *Nice colors but you wouldn't find them in my house.* Still she did like the look.

I bought stain for a wood project, herbs to plant in the garden, and supplies for an above-ground flower bed. I also purchased a metal shed where I could move my stuff from the garage. The shed came with 320 screws and an estimated 15 hour completion time. For me that translated to 45 hours since I'm slow. That's okay; I'm not going anywhere.

I even got my bike tuned up. And to add a voice to the house, I got one of those smart speakers. I'd say, "Alexa, play a Beatles playlist, or tell me a joke." Adding her voice to the silence lightened my mood.

I began telling my friends how Alexa and I would argue. She'd complain when I didn't vacuum and I'd tell her that was her responsibility. She'd counter, "Oh, so it's my fault?" And she nagged me if I left my socks in the middle of the room.

A little humor during a pandemic goes a long way.

Like everyone else, I stocked up on food and I even bought an air fryer to make low fat crunchy things. Now I was all set for Armageddon.

As the weeks went on, I became distracted and distanced from my grief. With the world spinning and concerns about my health and those of my family and friends, I didn't say goodbye to my grief or to Susan, but the dissonance around me grew louder. Here was one more difficult experience I had to endure without the love of my life.

What happened with Susan was suddenly old news to the people around me as other concerns got in the way. Life gets crowded.

My friends still asked how my children and I were doing, but not as often. This heightened my sadness and loneliness, but I knew I had to push forward. I didn't want to fall back into the pit of despair I worked so hard to climb out from. Susan would not want that for me. So I signed up for a college course online and planned FaceTime and Zoom calls.

Perhaps the best change came when I reconnected with people from my past. I went on Facebook and LinkedIn searching for old friends once cherished but with whom I'd lost contact. We talked about loves and losses, successes and failures. We talked about spouses, children and grandchildren.

Every call ended with, "I'm so glad we reconnected; let's stay in touch." My world was now expanding a bit and none of this would have happened if it wasn't for a pandemic. I would trade it all for one more hug and kiss from Susan, but that wasn't going to happen, so I needed to seize whatever benefit I could grasp.

The pandemic was a wake-up call, demonstrating that life is like a moving sidewalk. If you don't move with it, you end up going backward. I'd been through too much to go backward or stand still any longer.

Bad things will always continue to happen. You could get coronavirus or be hit by a truck. You could lose another loved one or all the above.

The pandemic hit me like a tsunami, slapping me across my face and saying, "Steve, enough. Get your act together and start living already."

For others, the turning point might be something good and gentle that touches your heart and soul. Maybe there will be a new "meant to be" person you never envisioned you'd meet. Perhaps you'll find a new rewarding project, job or hobby. These options are all more appealing than a pandemic.

But whatever nudges you, it's important to move forward. If something external doesn't come and push you, take it upon yourself to join a club, take a class, get a new job, or find a new calling. In other words, rewrite the script of your life. Not the entire book, just a few chapters. You'll find people love a come-from-behind victory. They inevitably cheer when the underdog wins.

Susan and I climbed to the top of a beautiful mountain together. Then we descended from the summit. I finally climbed out of the valley, finding myself without her on a new road never traveled before.

A new road can be scary. But I believe with energy, strength and conviction, each of us can chart a new positive path.

"*Yesterday I was clever, so I wanted to change the world. Today I am wise, so I am changing myself.*"

—Jalaluddin Mevlana Rumi

IF YOU KNOW SOMEONE WHO LOST A SPOUSE OR OTHER LOVED ONE

"If you want happiness for an hour, take a nap. If you want happiness for a day, go fishing. If you want happiness for a year, inherit a fortune. If you want happiness for a lifetime, help someone else."—Proverb

Advice on how to help your friend or neighbor after the loss of their loved one:

Suppose you're in the supermarket and you run into a neighbor who just lost their spouse. You've lived near each other for ten years and share the same street. You know the person to say hello, but your friendship has never gone beyond casual conversation or friendly waves.

Maybe someone down the hall at work is suffering a loss. Word around the office is that the person is hurting. You've worked on a few projects together, maybe even had a beer together after work, but you're not close.

These are just two in a myriad of possible scenarios. The point is we all recognize other people's pain, even from a distance, but we often feel awkward and at a loss for words when we want to help or show compassion.

So what to do? The simple answer is to just show up. Maybe even admit you don't know what to say. But spend a little extra time either making small talk or listening to the other person. Listening is often the best gift we can give someone, especially in this situation.

If you want to go a little further, mention you like a nearby Starbucks and ask the person if he or she wants to join you for coffee. By reaching out, you make a difference for the other person, whether they accept your offer or not.

Keep in mind that telling the other person to call if they need anything is a standard means of outreach that's almost worthless. Chances are close to zero that a person in a grieving state will call someone they don't know particularly well. Your intentions may be good, but the execution is weak. You may be sincere, but don't put the onus on someone in grief to reach out to you.

If they say no to coffee, or to sitting on your porch and chatting, don't take offense. Just make the offer again after a few weeks. Even if it never happens, your outreach will be appreciated. Remember you are reaching out to them, not the other way around.

Other gestures might be to bring a potted plant for your office mate's desk with a card of condolence. Shoveling a neighbor's walk or putting their trash cans back where they're kept after the trash person empties them are kind ways of helping in a subtle way without making the person feel indebted.

If you do have coffee, or lunch, or just a chat with the person, don't ask probing questions. Let the grieving person reveal as much or as little as he or she finds comfortable. Your role is not to satisfy your curiosity, but to help someone with a broken heart. The gesture of helping is a blessing to both of you.

If you're so inclined, offer to do grocery shopping for the person who is grieving. Or suggest getting together to watch an old movie and order a pizza.

Avoid all the trite expressions: *He (or she) is in a better place. The Almighty has a plan for her. Don't think about what you lost, think about what you had. His (or her) suffering is over.*

Make sure to display patience with a person in grief. They are hurt and it will take time for them to return to something resembling normal. Don't tell them "time's up" either—everyone grieves at their own pace.

After all, everyone is different and situations vary. While there are commonalities, the process of acceptance and moving forward is a challenge without a timetable.

Empathize but don't compare your losses with theirs.

Allow the survivor to talk about their deceased loved one when they're ready to share. But don't push them to reveal more than their comfort level allows.

Once the person opens up, don't be surprised if they repeat themselves or tell you the same stories more than once. They are processing loss and this is how many come to terms with what has happened.

"The only way to have a friend is to be one."
—Ralph Waldo Emerson

PARTING THE RIGHT WAY

"Even a happy life cannot be without a measure of darkness, and the word happy would lose its meaning if it were not balanced by sadness."—Carl Jung

If you take time and effort to care for each other, you as the survivor will be able to rebuild in an easier manner.

This is not, by any means, an easy task. But it definitely helps that Susan and I closed out our time together loving each other more than at any other time. My heart is broken but I feel proud of our marriage from first day to last.

I can rebuild with a clear conscience, without the guilt and remorse many feel, for I am proud how we landed.

Life is anything but perfect. The key to making it through is accepting what you cannot change and developing an attitude of finding or building a workaround for whatever stands in the way.

"The moments we share are the moments we keep forever."—unknown

ENDNOTE

Susan and I had a wonderful marriage, with our love built on various principles:

It's better to be happy than right.

Argue behind closed doors, without involving kids or anyone else.

Start and end each day with a hug, a kiss, and the words, "I love you."

Never take each other for granted, not even for a moment.

Make sure your favorite place is next to each other.

Together joys are doubled and sorrows cut in half.

My wish for everyone is that you find your soulmate and treasure that person for however long you are fortunate to have each other.

I was lucky enough and smart enough to have Susan in my life for 41 years. When it is right, like it was for us, no amount of time is enough. But the time we had will have to do, for I promised Susan I would go on. And I'm not about to start breaking my promises to her now.

—*Steven Shefter*